BARRIER ISLANDS ARE FOR THE BIRDS

BY LARRY POINTS & ANDREA JAUCK

SIERRA PRESS
Mariposa, CA

ISBN 1-58071-023-9

Printed in Singapore, First Edition; Spring 2000
Designed by Sullivan Santamaria Design, Flagstaff, AZ

The authors express deep appreciation to all the researchers, friends and colleagues who contributed photographs to this book.

PHOTO CREDITS - BARRIER ISLANDS ARE FOR THE BIRDS

National Park Service (NPS) file photos: Page 4, (aerial view); page 11, center; page 14, top; page 23, bottom right; page 27, center (shorebirds feeding).

U.S. Fish & Wildlife Service (USFWS) file photos: page 12, center; page 19, right; page 28, top left.

Corel Corporation: Page 16, both bottom images.

Tracy Ammerman: Page 21 (laughing gull colony).

Christine Bauman (NPS): Page 14, bottom.

Maggie Briggs (NPS): Page 21 (kingbird in high marsh).

Dave Brinker: Page 15, bottom; page 23 (green heron chicks); page 28, bottom.

Roger Clapp (USFWS): page 13, bottom right (black skimmer's head); page 26, top; page 28, center.

Michael Colopy: page 7, top; page 8, top left; page 17, top right (kestral); page 18, all images; page 19, top (great horned owl) and center (broad-winged hawk); page 20, top left (red-tailed hawk); page 22, all images; page 30, top (old squaws).

William T. Drennen: page 23, top right (adult green heron).

Allen Deward: page 27, bottom.

D.H. Ellis (USFWS): page 19, bottom.

Middleton Evans: page 3, top right (pelican); page 10, bottom left; page 25, right; page 26 (oyster catchers); page 28, top right (egret feeding young); page 29, bottom right.

Dan Fleischer (NPS): page 7, bottom left (gull in sand).

Richard Frear (NPS): page 12, top; page 24, bottom.

Larry Hindman (Maryland Department of Natural Resources): page 30, bottom.

Ed Huberty: page 5 (osprey in flight); page 9, bottom; page 13 (adult skimmers in sand); page 23, left; page 24, top; page 25, left; page 29, top right; page 30 (mute swan and tern).

Kevin Karlson: page 9, top inset.

Craig Koppie (USFWS): Back Cover, (peregrine falcon).

Laurie MacIvor: page 11, bottom.

Lynn Troy Maniscalco: page 1 ("So many birds").

Bill Maynard (NPS): page 21 (clapper rail).

Len McKenzie (NPS): page 10, top.

J. Kent Minichiello: Front Cover, bottom right (American avocet); page 8, right (full scenic); page 9, center; page 13 (skimmers in flight); page 17, bottom right (yellow-rumped warbler); page 20, bottom right; page 26 (American avocet).

C. Mukczek (USFWS): page 21, bottom (herring gull chicks).

Gordon Noreau (NPS): page 12, bottom.

Marion Pohlman (USFWS): page 27, top (horseshoe crabs).

Beverly Points: page 3, left (ranger with kids).

Larry Points: page 7, bottom right (gull on fence post); page 15, top left (kite) and right (dog); page 16, top (swallows in flight); page 32.

Margaret Rafal: page 26 (black-necked stilt).

Bruce Rogers (NPS): page 20 (aerial view of marsh).

Marian Sargeant: Front Cover, bottom center (great blue heron).

Herb Sargeant: page 2; page 3, right center (gull) and bottom right (skimmer); page 29, center.

Ted Swem (USFWS): page 15, top center (peregrin falcon).

Allison Turner (NPS): page 24, center.

Jerry Via: Front Cover, bottom left (Laughing gull); page 4, top left inset; page 10, center (royal tern colony); page 11, top; page 13, (chicks with eggs); page 15 (tern chicks).

Harvey Wickwire (NPS): page 5, (full aerial view).

M.W. Williams (NPS): page 6, bottom right.

Robert E. Wilson (USFWS): page 31

Michael Yates: Page 16, top left (swallows resting in dunes).

Carl Zimmerman: Front Cover (barrier island aerial view); page 5, right (ospreys on nest); page 6, top; page 10, bottom right; page 17, left (full scenic) and right center (dead snag).

To young birders everywhere
and their joy of discovery.

From a bird's-eye-view, a *barrier island* stretches out like a long, narrow ribbon of sand surrounded by bright blue water. It is a wild, special world that forms only where the land and sea come together. Islands are always changing with the power of ocean wind and waves, but for many birds, these fragile bits of land are home. An island's secluded beaches and marshes are ideal places to raise young. Every year, thousands of birds seek out islands as safe havens to rest and feed during long migrations.

Barrier islands are low strips of sand and mud along the Atlantic and Gulf coasts, separated from the mainland by a shallow bay. They are called "barriers" because they protect the mainland from ocean storms and flooding. Other shoreline barriers, such as *capes* (like Cape Cod in Massachusetts) and long *peninsulas* (like Sandy Hook near New York City) are very similar to islands, although they are attached to the mainland at one end. Most of these barriers share the same kinds of habitats and wildlife. Coastal birds need safe habitats where they can rest, feed and take care of their young.

An **osprey** may fly over the beach, dunes, forests, salt marshes and other island habitats on its way to catch fish in the ocean or bay. Ospreys, or "fish hawks," are great hunters. They have excellent eyesight and can spot fish swimming just below the surface from over 100 feet in the air. Then they swoop quickly down into the water and grab the fish with their very strong, sharp *talons,* or claws. Ospreys also have spines on the soles of their toes to help them hold on to wriggling, slippery prey.

Ospreys carry fish to huge nests high on top of trees, boat channel markers or other man-made platforms where their hungry chicks await. Every year, an osprey pair returns to the very same nest they used the year before. Even if the nest is large, the male and female will continue building on it each spring. Soon the nest is an enormous pile of branches, ropes, fishing lines, tin cans and anything else the ospreys can carry. Two long snake skeletons were even found in one nest!

Although it looks calm under a golden sunrise, the beach is a harsh habitat for most animals. In winter, storm waves pound the shore and an icy wind blows. In summer, the sand can be incredibly hot. Yet beaches always seem filled with **gulls** busy searching the sand for food or resting together in large groups. Gulls are the most familiar birds along the shore, and it's hard to imagine the beach without their noisy cries. In fact, beaches would be smelly, uninviting places for people if gulls didn't constantly clean up dead animals and debris brought in by the waves.

Gulls are scavengers of the beach and they eat anything they can find, dead or alive. They also hunt for small animals and even like to eat tasty clams—but clam shells are too hard to peck open. Instead some gulls carry the clams up into the air and drop them on a hard surface like a road (or even a car!) to crack them open.

Gulls are easy for young birdwatchers to observe. They group together in large flocks out in the open and stay in place for a long time. Gulls can be seen sleeping, eating, preening (cleaning their feathers) or interacting with each other. However, they can be difficult to identify. Young gulls display a bewildering variety of mottled brown and grey patterns. Depending on the species, it takes from one to four years for young gulls to look like their parents.

Adult gulls have certain distinct markings. The noisy **laughing gull** has a jet black head in summer and a speckled black and white head in winter. The **herring gull** has a yellow bill with a bright red spot. Herring gull chicks peck at this spot to get the parents to feed them. **Great black-backed gulls,** the largest gulls along the coast, have very dark colored feathers. Gulls and other coastal birds often have darker backs than bellies. This helps them escape predators both in the air and the sea. Gulls blend in with the dark ocean water when seen from above, and match the light sky when seen from below.

Energetic little **sanderlings** feed right where waves are crashing. Sanderlings and other kinds of sandpipers dart back and forth at the water's edge. They probe the wet sand with their long bills, snatching up bits of food brought in by the ocean. They also search for tiny coquina clams and mole crabs that actually live in the sand at the surf line.

A sandpiper does a lot of hopping and resting on one leg. The other leg is tucked under the body, usually to help the sandpiper stay warm. In a chilly sea breeze, birds like **dunlins** can lose heat through thin legs not covered by feathers.

Sandpipers are part of a group of birds called **shorebirds.** Shorebirds spend a lot of time on islands, especially during migration. They are terrific flyers and some species travel thousands of miles each year between arctic nesting grounds and tropical wintering grounds. Along the way, they stop at islands to rest and feed for the long journey ahead. The best time to see these huge shorebird flocks is during the peak of migration in late spring and early fall.

Shorebirds have long bills, plump bodies and thin, stick-like legs. Those with longer legs will wade into shallow bays and marshes, but many shorebirds barely come close enough to the water to get their toes wet.

The *wrack line* is the highest point on the beach reached by waves during high tide. Shells, seaweed, driftwood, tiny sea creatures and other wrack, or debris, tend to pile up there. Hungry shorebirds, including the colorful **ruddy turnstone, black-bellied plover** and large **willet,** search the wrack for food. The turnstone gets its name from the way it turns over stones with its bill when feeding. The willet is named for its loud "pill-will-willet" call it repeats as it flies.

But where is the plover's black belly? Like many birds, the plover changes color from winter to summer. In summer's *breeding plumage,* its belly becomes jet black and the top of its head turns snow white.

Shorebirds share the wrack line with all kinds of birds. A dead horseshoe crab makes a good meal for a **boat-tailed grackle,** a noisy blackbird with an unusually long, broad tail.

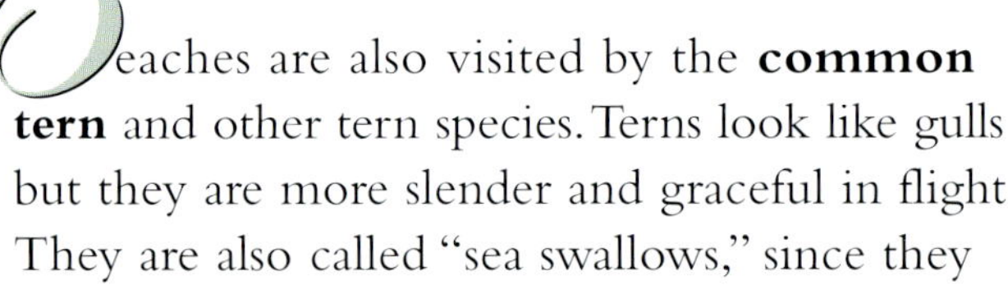

Beaches are also visited by the **common tern** and other tern species. Terns look like gulls but they are more slender and graceful in flight. They are also called "sea swallows," since they have swallow-like, forked tails. Like the osprey, a tern snatches food from the water, but it dives in and grabs fish with its sharp bill, not talons. The tern then gulps the fish head-first so the pointy scales don't stick in its throat.

Most species, including the **royal tern,** nest on the back part of wide, broad beaches, away from the ocean. They gather in large *colonies,* or groups, because there is safety in numbers. Any unwanted intruder is greeted by a squad of angry adult terns that swoop, scream and dive. Some even *regurgitate,* or throw up, on the invader's head!

A large colony is a noisy, confusing place for chicks and their parents. Adults have to learn to recognize their own chicks by sight and by sound. Royal tern chicks each have a different color pattern in their feathers, beaks and feet to help their parents find them in the bustling, crowded colony—or after the chicks have been banded and released by careful scientists.

Many scientists up and down the coast are also trying to help a special bird called the **piping plover.** These small shorebirds nest high up on the beach, like terns, but they don't gather in colonies. Instead each pair finds an isolated spot in the sand to make a *scrape,* or nest. Piping plovers are endangered because safe, secluded beaches are getting harder to find. To help them, biologists place large cages over nests and eggs. The birds can easily get in and out of these cages, but hungry foxes, raccoons and gulls cannot.

Plover chicks are ready to run and feed as soon as they hatch. Then all the birds leave their protective cage. The light-colored plovers blend in well with the sand, which helps them hide from their enemies. However, if an enemy does wander too close, the adult will try to lead it away by "piping" loudly and pretending to have a hurt wing. Most predators will follow an injured animal, hoping for an easy meal. Once the predator has been lured far enough away, the plover will suddenly "recover" and fly back to its young.

The dune habitat begins far back on the beach where blowing sand collects around a clump of grass. Any obstacle, such as a plant, piece of driftwood or man-made fence can trap sand and build dunes. Dunes are similar to a hot, dry desert. Secretive dune residents come out during the cooler evening hours, leaving only their tracks behind in the daytime.

Away from crashing waves and blowing wind, dunes are quiet, secluded places. Birds often sleep or nest in the low areas between dunes where they feel hidden and secure. Dunes are important to islands and other coastal barriers because they block stormy ocean waves from flooding the inland habitats.

Many seashore areas prohibit people from walking on dunes. If enough plants are killed or disturbed, the fragile dunes erode away—and birds like the **horned lark** will lose a grassy nesting site.

Beautiful **black skimmers** guard their nests or stretch out for a nap among the dune and beach plants. Skimmers, relatives of terns, also lay eggs right in the sand. Birds that nest in the open have to sit for hours on their eggs and chicks to keep them out of the hot sun.

The black skimmer gets its name from the spectacular way it catches fish. The skimmer flies low, or *skims,* over the water with its lower bill held just below the surface. When the bill touches a fish or other small animal, it automatically snaps up and grabs the prey. Skimmers have unique eyes to help them feed at night. In fact, they are one of the few birds with eyes that can become vertical slits, like a cat's, and then enlarge at night to gather in very dim light. Without these "cat's eyes," skimmers might fly right into a pier!

The black skimmer's very long lower bill is constantly wearing away as the bird feeds. To keep up with the rate of wear, the lower bill actually grows faster than the upper bill.

Birds that nest on the beach and among the dunes face certain dangers. Storms can wash away whole colonies of beach nests and even flood the dunes. The most powerful waves might *overwash* the island, carrying sand from the beach across the island and into the bay. Entire habitats can be forever changed in a few hours. This seems destructive, but storms and flooding are a natural part of barrier island life. Birds and other wildlife have learned to adapt to these dynamic forces. If nests are lost early enough in the season, most birds will have time to lay a second *clutch,* or group of eggs, and try again.

An even greater danger comes from humans who visit barrier islands and build houses along the coast. As more and more people enjoy the seashore, there are less isolated beaches and dunes for nesting birds. Visitors should keep far away from any colony or nesting site. Birds are easily disturbed by people walking, driving or even sunbathing too close to their nests. Dogs running loose can do great damage to a colony of terns.

Even kite-flying can be a problem. Certain kites hovering in the breeze resemble a fierce **peregrine falcon,** which is a predator of smaller birds. If birds are constantly scared off their nests, they can't protect their eggs and chicks from predators or from the broiling sun.

Litter is also a danger for birds. Chicks can get tangled in fishing line or stuck in bottles and cans. The smell of litter attracts predators to nesting sites. Everyone needs to help keep seashores clean and safe for the animals that live there.

Farther inland, away from the ocean, the open dunes give way to thickets of hardy shrubs and vines. The shrub habitat offers small birds shelter from the weather and sharp-eyed predators, and the abundant plant life harbors lots of insects that birds need to feed their young.

Island shrubs also provide birds with a bounty of nutritious berries in the fall. On barrier islands with dense stands of bayberry, a common shrub along the mid-Atlantic coast, beach goers are treated to a stunning autumn sight. Huge masses of migrating **tree swallows** descend upon these bushes, eating thousands of waxy bayberries and resting among the dunes. Then they leave as quickly as they come, tumbling south in large flocks to spend the winter in tropical habitats.

As their name suggests, tree swallows nest in hollow tree cavities and human-built boxes. Their more urban cousins, **barn swallows,** attach nests made of mud under building eaves and rafters. Barn swallows feed their chicks a tremendous amount of insects during the summer, including thousands of barrier island mosquitoes.

The zone where dunes and shrubs meet the maritime, or coastal forest is one of the most diverse *ecotones* on a barrier island. An ecotone is the place where two different habitats come together and overlap their borders. The rich combination of flowering plants, berry-laden vines, trees, shrubs and grasses along this ecotone acts like a magnet for birds and birdwatchers. The beautiful **American kestrel,** a small colorful falcon, can be seen searching for rodents, birds and grasshoppers in the open areas among blooming goldenrods and bushy thickets.

The edge of the forest facing the ocean is marked by stunted, odd-shaped trees with twisted branches. These trees have been pruned into strange forms by salt spray in the wind, which is harmful to certain plants. Oaks, maples, sassafras, and other large-leafed trees hunker low under tall protective pine trees such as loblolly and pitch pine, which can tolerate more salt. The **yellow-rumped warbler** is one of many songbirds that flits through the salt-pruned trees and shrubs. It searches for insects in summer and feasts on bayberries in winter.

In the deepest part of a barrier island forest, the ocean seems far away. Wind in the trees replaces the sound of waves. The air smells like pine and soil instead of salt. Hidden by overhead leaves, forest birds are usually heard before they are seen. A persistent "meow" coming from above is the alarm call of a **gray catbird,** a lively, curious bird that sounds remarkably like a cat up a tree! Catbirds also create complex melodies that mimic the songs of other birds. They eat the berries of almost all barrier island shrubs and vines, including poison ivy, wild grape and thorny "catbriar."

On the forest floor, the well-camouflaged **woodcock** uses its sensitive long bill to probe for earthworms in the soil. **Bobwhite quail** nibble leaves and scratch the ground for seeds and berries. Like birds that nest on the beach, the quail and the woodcock blend perfectly into the environment. Their woodland color patterns make them almost invisible until they are flushed from cover.

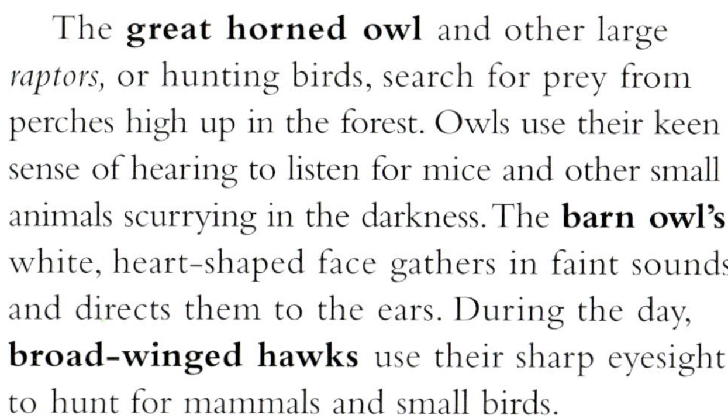

The **great horned owl** and other large *raptors,* or hunting birds, search for prey from perches high up in the forest. Owls use their keen sense of hearing to listen for mice and other small animals scurrying in the darkness. The **barn owl's** white, heart-shaped face gathers in faint sounds and directs them to the ears. During the day, **broad-winged hawks** use their sharp eyesight to hunt for mammals and small birds.

Years ago, large birds at the top of the food chain, like the **bald eagle,** were poisoned by a pesticide called DDT that weakened their egg

shells. The eggs broke when the parents sat on them, and the developing young birds died. Since DDT was banned in the United States in 1972, populations of eagles, ospreys, falcons, hawks and pelicans have increased. Today, young eaglets and other raptors thrive on barrier islands all along the coast.

A **red-tailed hawk** may be found soaring over a lush salt marsh, one of nature's most productive habitats. A salt marsh is a grassy meadow partly covered by salt water at high tide. These wet grasslands develop on the back side of barrier islands and usually border a calm, shallow bay. Marsh grass is constantly growing, dying and decaying. Microscopic bits of decayed grass, called *detritus,* end up in the bay where they feed vast numbers of young fish, clams and shrimp. Some scientists think that the salt marsh food chain helps support most of the animal life in the northern Atlantic Ocean.

During high tide, bay water moves deep into the marsh through snake-like *guts,* or channels. As the tide recedes, large amounts of detritus are carried out into the bay. Shallow pools left behind in the grass trap minnows and small crabs, which attract many hungry wading birds. Once considered worthless, these beautiful wetlands are important food factories. Countless birds, mammals, fish and tiny sea creatures live and feed among the grasses.

The upper, or high marsh is bordered by small shrubs like marsh elder and groundsel that can tolerate some salt water. This part of the marsh is higher in elevation and drier than the low marsh near the bay. Only the highest tides or bay storms bring salt water this far inland. An **eastern kingbird** keeps watch for flying insects, its main summer food. Along with many other birds that nest in the United States, the kingbird migrates to Central America where it spends the winter in rainforest habitats that, unfortunately, are slowly disappearing.

The secretive **clapper rail** nests deep in the grass and is rarely seen. The saying "thin as a rail" comes from the bird's amazing ability to slip between marsh grasses and quickly disappear from sight. Several bird species nest in the marsh where the dense hay-like grass makes ideal cover and helps hide chicks from predators.

Just a few inches of elevation are enough to create a dry nesting site for a colony of laughing gulls. A short time after pecking out of its shell, a gull chick will become soft and downy.

The calm and stately **great blue heron** is easy to watch as it carefully stalks its prey along the marsh edge. Nearly four feet tall, this graceful wader is one of the largest birds found on a barrier island. A great blue heron often stands perfectly still for long periods of time with its long neck curled back and dagger-like bill poised ready to strike. When the bird's sharp eyes spot movement, the bill stabs quickly—and a fish, crab, small mammal, young bird or even a snake is quickly snatched up and swallowed whole!

Many kinds of herons feed in salt marshes and freshwater island ponds. They are usually easy to tell apart by size, color and behavior. The **little blue heron** is smaller and darker blue than its large relative. It also tends to feed alongside other wading birds; the solitary great blue heron prefers to hunt alone.

The **tricolored heron** is about the same size as a little blue heron but it has a white belly and dark reddish feathers mixed in with its blue feathers. This energetic heron rushes back and forth in shallow water, waving its wings and stirring up the bottom with its long toes. It actively chases its prey instead of patiently standing and waiting.

The shy **green heron** blends in well with a background of grass and leaves, although it often appears more bluish brown than green. Unlike its comical babies, the adult's long neck is usually only visible when the bird lunges for a fish.

Short and chunky, the **black-crowned night-heron** feeds late in the evening when other herons are in their *roosts,* or sleeping places high in the trees. This patient hunter is a master at the watch-and-wait method of feeding. It often stands so completely still that it looks like a statue. Young birdwatchers can easily see its dark red eyes through binoculars.

Handsome white egrets often gather with herons in the salt marsh. The word *egret* means "small heron," although the **great egret** is almost as tall as the great blue heron. Look for its yellowish bill and long black legs. Smaller and more active, the black-billed **snowy egret** has bright yellow feet that it shakes in the water to stir up the bottom and perhaps attract curious fish.

Wild horses live on several barrier islands, particularly Assateague Island in Maryland and Virginia. They have a special relationship with **cattle egrets,** small white herons long associated with Africa's great herds of grazing animals. Cattle egrets somehow crossed the Atlantic Ocean in the late 1800s, landed in South America and spread north. Their partnership with grazing animals continues today. Cattle egrets pick bothersome insects off the horses' coats; in return, the horses kick up more insects than the birds can find on their own.

Both egrets and herons are easy to identify in flight. They pull their long necks tightly in and trail their thin legs behind them. They also flap their wings in a slow, steady rhythm.

Herons and egrets, especially snowy egrets, were almost hunted to extinction in the late 1800s for the beautiful feathers they display during the breeding season. These feathers were greatly prized as decorations for ladies' hats. People became alarmed at how many birds were being killed just for the sake of fashion. Eventually laws were passed that protected most birds from being killed for their feathers. Wildlife refuges and national seashores helped provide safe places for wading birds to live, and today their populations have greatly recovered.

The **white ibis** is another marsh bird that was once hunted for its feathers. The ibis looks like a great egret, but it has a red down-curved bill it uses to probe the mud for small crabs and other marine creatures. White ibises are usually found only in the southern states, although some wander northward in summer. The more common **glossy ibis** looks almost black from a distance. Unlike herons and egrets, ibises fly with both legs and necks outstretched.

The wide bay beyond the salt marsh attracts great flocks of birds with its abundant aquatic life. Shallow water and mud flats exposed at low tide are especially popular shorebird feeding sites. Different species can eat together because each one has its own feeding method. Some shorebirds probe deep in the mud for soft worms. Several like to catch fish in very shallow water; others prefer it deeper. Certain birds search for prey near the surface, while a few feed only near the bottom.

Each shorebird has a bill shaped for its own special way of eating. The **American oystercatcher** uses its thin reddish-orange bill to slice into oysters and clams when they partly open their shells to feed.

Bills are very important to all birds. They take the place of hands and are used for holding, carrying, digging, feeding, fighting and nest-building. Bills also help with bird identification. The **black-necked stilt** has a straight, needle-shaped bill for probing the bay bottom. The similar **avocet** has an unusual upturned bill that it swings from side to side in the water to stir up creatures hidden in the mud.

Along the Atlantic coast, migrating shorebirds have a remarkable relationship with one of the ocean's oddest creatures—the horseshoe crab. Gentle horseshoe crabs are not really crabs at all. They are ancient creatures that roamed the ocean when dinosaurs walked the earth. Ticks and spiders are their closest relatives today.

Each spring, thousands of horseshoe crabs come ashore and lay millions of eggs. Most gather on secluded beaches along the Delaware Bay. Rusty colored **red knots** and other hungry shorebirds depend on these eggs to help fuel their long journey to arctic breeding grounds. Red knots fly 5,000 miles before stopping at the Delaware Bay. Exhausted and starving, they gorge on the tiny green eggs for nearly two weeks. Each bird can eat as many as 130,000 eggs.

In the late 1990s, biologists noticed an alarming decline in the horseshoe crab population. They were once harvested by the ton for use as fertilizer. Then fishermen chopped them up as bait for their eel pots, or traps. Today, many concerned people are trying to protect Atlantic horseshoe crabs. Their survival is essential to over a million shorebirds that depend on them.

Small islands in the bay make ideal *rookeries,* or group nesting sites. Many water birds choose uninhabited islands for nesting because they are free from foxes, raccoons, snakes and other predators. Egrets and herons often share a crowded rookery in a clump of bushes or small trees. Each bird has its own spot in the rookery "apartment building," with the larger birds on top. Chicks are born helpless and must be cared for a long time. Parents usually feed their young by regurgitating half-digested fish. Rookeries are very noisy, smelly places!

Brown pelicans also nest in rookeries as far north as Maryland, and are sometimes seen flying even farther north. Brown pelicans are fun to watch when they dive for food. Their huge bills and expandable throat pouches are perfectly shaped for scooping up fish like a net. The pelican fills its pouch with nearly three gallons of fish and water. The bill tips down to drain the water, then up to gulp the fish.

More than any other bird, a pelican chick looks like a reptile—and supports the idea that birds evolved from dinosaurs.

Turkey vultures soar over island habitats looking and even smelling for *carrion,* or dead animals to scavenge. On chilly mornings, they often stand with their enormous wings outstretched to absorb heat from the sun.

The **anhinga** is another large, strange-looking bird that stands with its silvery-black wings spread. Unlike most water birds, anhingas don't have waterproof feathers. After diving deep to catch fish, they stand in the sun to dry off and get warm. Anhingas are only found in the far southern states since they lose body heat rapidly in colder water.

Double-crested cormorants, relatives of anhingas, live all along the shore in summer. Cormorants are skilled divers that grab fish with their hooked bills. Once they get waterlogged, cormorants also have to stand in the sun and spread their soaked feathers to dry. Cormorants occasionally share rookeries with herons and egrets. On hot days, they spread their wings over the nest to keep their black chicks from absorbing too much sun.

From summer to winter, birds take turns sharing barrier islands. As the days get shorter, most shore and wading birds slowly head south. Their place is taken by ducks, geese and other waterfowl looking for safe places to rest and feed during migration. Groups of hardy sea ducks, such as **oldsquaw,** can be seen bobbing up and down or flying low over cold ocean waves.

Some waterfowl will spend the entire winter in island wetlands as long as there is water free of ice. The **American wigeon** and other dabbling ducks paddle around shallow marshes and eat underwater plants. Healthy, protected wetlands are very important to the survival of many wintering birds.

Several kinds of waterfowl live year-round on islands. With so many birds sharing these small bits of land, relationships between different species are not always peaceful. The beautiful, but aggressive **mute swan** was brought by humans from Europe and is expanding its range south. It chases and even attacks native birds, which disturbs their ability to nest or feed. Biologists are studying what impact these swans and other foreign birds have on native bird populations.